I0420885

365 Page Personal Diary

Printed in the United States

ISBN-13: 978-1519273789

ISBN-10: 1519273789

This book belongs to: ______________________

If found please call:________________________

Email:_____________________________________

© sommai – US.Fotolia.com

All Write All Bright Books
71 Tandy Lane
Sparta, TN 38583
(931)946-1221

www.ingramcontent.com/pod-product-compliance
Lightning Source LLC
Chambersburg PA
CBHW071327280526
45787CB00001B/19
9781519273789